Politics, Prophesy, and Prostitution

by
Dr. G. J. Curts

authorHOUSE®

AuthorHouse™
1663 Liberty Drive, Suite 200
Bloomington, IN 47403
www.authorhouse.com
Phone: 1-800-839-8640

First published by AuthorHouse   9/24/2007

ISBN: 978-1-4343-3866-2 (sc)

Library of Congress Control Number: 2007907031

Printed in the United States of America
Bloomington, Indiana

This book is printed on acid-free paper.

Table Of Contents

"My people perish

for

lack of knowledge ... "

- Hosea -

Dedication

This book is dedicated to the memory of following friends

and

family members.

Emily Berg

Beatrice Kelley Gillispie

RoseAnna Gumbinger

Ethel J. Slater Pepper

Joyce Gwendolyn Pepper

Webster C. Pepper

Dr. Ira L. Slater

and to the memory of all patriots
who upheld the Constitution,
the Bill of Rights
and
loved this land
we call
the United States of America.

Acknowledgement

I appreciate and am grateful to my friend
Hazel Pace Martin. She has championed
my creative gifts in poetry since we were
 kids in High School. She continues to be
a steadfast motivator. Without her
encouragement and belief in my talent
through the years this book would not
have been written.

I am deeply indebted to my dear friend
Mivy Wise who's joy, enthusiasm, and
encouragement fanned the embers
of my efforts. She even bought books I
was published in.

A very special thank you to my editorial
team: Vicki Wooden and Henry Regnier.
They were excellent in immediate feed
back, corrections, and encouragement.
They lived with the process of this book
as much as I did. To them I am deeply
indebted.

Thank you!

The Author

I am an ordinary person who had some extra ordinary opportunities such as a college education which began at Washtenaw Community College in Michigan. It was here that my education began in political science.

Then I attended Northeast Missouri State University, (now known as Truman University,) obtaining a bachelor's degree. This experience added education, sociology, psychology as well as the sciences and arts.

I completed a M. S. N. degree in psychiatrics in conjunction with attending several institutes to developing therapeutic modalities for use in private practice. During this period I maintained a private practice and taught for several Universities and Colleges.

My Doctorate degree was earned at Chicago Theological Seminary where I developed a ministry to nurses, wrote a book called, <u>The Presence, The Unicorn, and Tree-be-hand</u>, served as a pastor, and hospital chaplain.

Since receiving my doctoral degree I continued to be active in all of the above. All of these experiences have enhanced the richness of my life. I enjoyed each one and all the wonderful people the experiences brought into my life. And those not so wonderful.

I have predominately lived in the Mid-West and the West my entire life. I have served my Native American cousins as well as my other cousins. God bless them all.

Every ordinary person has been given a gift, a gift they are to develop and share or return to re - create creation. My gift, my assignment is writing. Therefore, I must. And I enjoy it. I hope you do too!

Dr. G. J. Curts

Backword

I placed a "Backword" in the front of this book for most
assuredly it is the result of two things:
1) reflection which can only take place if something has taken
    place.
2) and hopefully we learn from reflection and move "foreword"
    making a difference with different choices.

As we proceed let us look backwards to the events to reflect
on them. You may want to research them for yourself. You may
disagree with my point of view and my personal life choices.

That is fine with me because hopefully that is what America
is still about ... freedom and diversity.

Today I looked in one of my favorite books called Space, Time,
and Medicine by Dr. Larry Dossey and the forward written by Fritjof
Capra.   I found that the medical, insurance, science, and social
concerns expressed by them 22 years earlier still exist today in
greater crisis than before.

Remember that expression, "It can't get worse", well it is silly and
it is false. Of course anything can get worse. And it is.

If we fail to examine the cause, if we do not see the symptoms
then a cure cannot be sought for that which can kill us. A virus
more deadly than Aids is taking victims by the millions. Power,
and Greed, and Blindness.

They are inextricably interwoven with politics, prophesy, and
prostitution of today.

Dr. G. J. Curts

More About The

Author...

For Such A Time As This !

I was born when Europe went to war.
Soon my country entered war for peace.
Tokens, rations, a passion for winning.
Men, women, children: everyone pitched in.

The War was on everyone's lips.
A prayer for peace at dinner tables.
Bandages for our soldiers wounds
made in kitchens' of our homes.

We all had someone in our heart,
each soldier became part of our
family that was on the battlefield.
Under fire the foxhole, a uniting force.

These were turbulent times.
Times of uncertainty, of fear.
Times of sacrifice, courage, valor.
I was born for such a time as this!

Faith in God was very strong.
We trusted each other and
government too.
An imperfect nation shaping itself.
I was born for such a time as this!

World War II won. For a brief moment
in our history prosperity and peace,
at least for us on the world stage.
Internally, shaking was going on.

Men and women back from war,
working women return home? Jobs?
The rights of women and people
of color brought tension and riots.

For Such A Time As This! (con.)

Shaking and shaping the national spirit
with the labor and travail of birth pains,
with the breaking of waters,
spilling of blood, placenta cut,
Freedoms child born.

My best friend and I,
an anigma to our races.
Now things were as they should be,
We were born for such a time as this.

And there was war,
we fought for peace,
Korea, Vietnam,
Granada ...

A president with victory signs
shatter like broken glass
the trust in the hearts of
a loving people.

We move on.
We go to war for peace.
Desert Storm, Haiti,
Kosovo.

We move on,.
We go to war for peace,
but not to win the war.
Victories declared,
madmen left in power
who will have to be
delt with again.

For Such A Time As This! (con)

Rome under Caesar,
Germany under Hitler,
America under her presidents
all choose the symbol of the eagle
representing power.

We now police
over seventy countries
in the name of peace ...
leaving us vulnerable at home.

Greed is at a mighty peak.
We ransom our very soul
to turn a profit in a foreign land
that kills its citizens, has slaves.

They steal our secrets,
our own technology, may kill us.
We give them money to bribe them
so they will not threaten us.

The spoken word reconstructs
our universe making changes
that veil evil masking it as good.
But I was born for such a time as this!

Particle birth.
Baby born alive.
Brains sucked out.
No particle death!

No! Separate church and state.
No religious laws nor praying.
No moral guides nor measuring sticks.
No tolerance, no respect, no boundaries.

For Such A Time As This! (con)

Nature abhors a vacuum.
Faith both wanes and flames.
God defamed --- crucified again
as art in urine in a bottle.

Parentless children for
whatever reasons roam
the streets of life bruised,
bruising, and alone.

With no one to talk with,
no one to care, no one to guide,
the vortex of the vacuum filled
with violence and death.
Columbine.

The news reads like a fiction novel,
something from space.
We are sending folks to the moon,
while working families live in cars.

And the One World Order
now has a new name,
it will be cloaked in "global".
Global trade, peace, UN and NATO.

But I was born for such a time as this!

Privacy, a thing of the past.
The computer records
what I buy to eat and the
brand of paper I use while
sitting on my toilet seat.

Do I disappear. Do I give up.
I get discouraged but do not disappear.

For Such A Time As This! (con.)

I take breaks but do not give up.
I must finish my race to win my prize.

Fear not. Do not disappear.
Keep your eyes on the prize
that we both know is there.
Get caught up praising
the Prince of Peace.

See through the deceptions.
Work on in this vineyard
until Jesus comes,
Saying, knowing, and praying:

Thank you Lord that:
I was born for such a time as this!

NOW THE BOOK
BEGINS!

Atomic Cloud

The nuclear tide has turned.
The life, the breath of every living thing threatened.
Evidenced by cataclysmic forces and toxic mushroom clouds.
Shaking the foundations of nations and the security of planet earth.

The tide has turned. The power shifted. Earth groans. Trembles.
Deterrents once in place no longer work.
Old enemies are allies ... a world in turmoil.
Too much vigilance to keep? Or did we merely fall asleep until ...

The explosive power of new nations in the race reverberates ...
Fear and shock waves. Fear and shock waves. Fear and shock waves.
Fear and shock waves.   Fear and shock waves.
Fallout umbrellas earth.

China
India
Pakistan
Iran

Leaders scramble for a plan to stop the madness,
stop the race, shift the power, turn the tide,
rushing, hurrying, praying, shaping
a plan for world peace.

President Dwight D. Eisenhower 1961
Farewell Address to the Nation

The Military -- Industrail Complex

"This conjunction of an immense military establishment and a large arms industry is new to the American experience. The total influence -- -- economic, political, even spiritual -- -- is felt in every city, every State house, every office of the Federal government. We recognize the imperative need for this development. Yet we must not fail to comprehend its grave importance. Our toil , resources and livelihood are all involved; so is the very structure of our society.

In councils of government, we must guard against the acquisition of unwarranted influence, whether sought or unsought, by the military industrial complex. The potential for disastrous rise of misplaced power exists and will persist.

We must never let the weight of this combination endanger our liberties or the democratic process. We should take nothing for granted. Only an alert and knowledgeable citizenry can compel. the proper meshing of the huge industrial and military machinery of defense with our peaceful methods and goals, so that security and liberty may prosper together."

President John F. Kennedy
Commencement Address
at the
American University

June 10, 1963

"-- -- yet it is the most important topic
on earth: world peace.

What kind of peace do I mean?
What kind of peace do we seek?
Not Pax Americana enforced on the
world by American weapons of war.
Not the peace of the grave or
the security of the slave.
I am talking about genuine peace
that makes life on earth worth living,
the kind of peace that enables men
and nations to grow and to hope and
to build a better life for their children ---
not merely peace for Americans but
peace for all men and women --
not merely in our time but peace
for all time."

Coup d' etat and Dying Kings

Shots rang out in Texas
President John F. Kennedy: dead.

All plans for peace reversed.
A shadow government in place.
A green light for Viet Nam.
Now the military industry thrives.

Another man of peace, Martin Luther King, Jr.
shot dead. Non- violent peaceful marches ...
equality for all.

A nation stunned and numb with shattered dreams
of dying kings could not forget, could not move on.
They could not see nor hear. Just numb.

Then a shot rang out again. Presidential candidate
Robert Kennedy, peace maker, murdered too.

Always a lone and crazy shooter,
a sacrifial lamb, someone must fall,
making it appear a meaningless act of one,
securing the shadow government and
lucrative growth of the military industry.

Men of peace are a dangerous threat
and they are slain.   Profits of war are
great for a few ... the losses are great
for many. Men of peace, slain for money.

Good Patriots Act Responsibly

When good patriots act responsibly
Freedom is preserved.
The cost may be great in fortune,
in lives, in friendships but when
freedom lives the people are alive.

The conquering of Freedom
will not come from outside, but
from unchecked powers within.
It will be surrendered when we,
the watchmen on the wall sleep.
An evil stealth and toxic power
will snatch us in the night.

Watchmen, stay awake. Alert us
with your cries that we may grab
our weapons, the Bill of Rights, the
Constitution, bear our arms and fight.
Let us not find them gone when we
need to arm ourselves for then it is
too late. Prisoners without recourse.

Good patriots act responsibly
demand illegal laws repealed.
Illegal laws in practice are a form
of tyranny punishable by law.
Good patriots are empowered by
the "Law" and act responsibly.

Demand our worthless dollars
backed by nothing be turned again
to gold. When good patriots act
responsibly evil has no home
and freedom is preserved.

God, Help Liberty

The US stands for freedom, integrity, equality.
Every day citizens gave their lives for these principals.
It's leadership decrees justice on world nations.

Your eyes do not deceive you. Figures straight forward.
The pillars are wavering, unbalanced, and crooked.
Records of the 1998 pillars of present leadership reveal:

29	accused	spousal abuse
7	arrested	for fraud
19	accused	of bad checks
119	bankrupted	two+ business
3	arrested	for assault
71	no credit	bad credit
14	arrested	drug charges
8	arrested	shoplifting
21	defendants	in lawsuits
84	stopped 1998	drunk driving

They crank out the laws, make international policies
keeping their citizens and citizens of the world deceived.
In great showmanship they fight. Being guilty themselves ...

They gently impeach a perjured president freedom.
Who are these lawmaker that are lawbreakers running free?
They are the 535 members of the United States Congress.

PEACE

OSLO.
"You give us
territory, and we'll fight
terrorism from that territory." (Arafat)

Instead. Bombs explode. Hundreds wounded. Terrorism. Death.
Destruction. Rabin betrayed. Rabin dies. Confrontation dies.
Declaration of genocide. Target Israel. Violence. Chaos.
Yielded territories undefended. Continued terrorist attacks.

Eastroom, White House, October 23, 1998
The annihilation of Israel is withdrawn.
Israel and Palestine sign: underscoring
movement toward fulfillment of the Accord.

One said," ... in the advent of the new millennium, in Jerusalem,
let Christians, Islam, and Jews celebrate the birth of Jesus."
And then the participant invoked this prayer, "Peace Come!"
Hope for humanity. Harmony. Relief. A prophetic statement.

Eastroom, White House, May 4, 1999.
Final agreement : signing of
the Peace Accord.
Salome!

21st Millennium

Deception reins - Peace.
Wars and rumors of war - Peace.
Peace talks - Plans for war - Peace.
Earthquakes, famine, floods, and disease - Peace.

Biological and chemical warfare - Peace.
A sheep is cloned - human cloning laws - Peace.
Harvesting of fetus, embryos, and human organs - Peace.
Drugs, alcohol, and poverty abound - Peace.

Religious percussion murders equal to the holocaust - Peace.
China and US partners in wealth - slaves' labor - Peace.
Russia and US partners in space - watching earth - Peace.
No boundaries, open trade: Aids mad cow disease - Peace.

Institutions crumble: New alliances form - Peace.
Goods are numbered: Currency gone - Peace.
An earth divided or an earth united?   Peace.
Prophets, psychics, and messiahs increase - Peace.

Fallen immoral leaders lead - Peace.
Axis form : target Jerusalem - Peace.
Pray for Jerusalem!
Peace!

America at the Millennium

One
Nation
Under God

Manifest Destiny
Native American Genocide
Imprisoned -   Reservations

Black Slaves,   Chinese Labors
Women, children,   the poor exploited
Desert Storm rash and the agent orange

IRS   CIA, FBI, CDC, FDA, ATF, Area 51
Elite, powerful, politics, perjury, freedom
House, Senate codependents in Clintionism

Friend of Israel ?   Give up your land.
China stealing   Killing Christians
Aims missals   favored nation

" A   house divided   cannot stand."(Bible)
'A food stamp army   cannot fight.' (Curts)

"A people that values   its privileges above its
principles soon loses   both." (Eisenhower)
Pray for America   at the Millennium.

The Eagle's Flight

The eagle flies mid heaven
this pattern warning, warning
that something is amiss.

The eagle prefers high flight
on air currents souring.
Souring. A majestic creature.

He is a messenger of God
delivering a warning
to the people of this planet.

The eagle flies mid heaven
telling of events that are
yet to come.

He cries, 'Nuclear winter, deep
deep cold, clouds of insidious
smoke block sun from earth.

The eagle flies mid heaven
warning warning warning
those dwelling on the earth.

If they change their behavior
the eagle will change flight.

The One World Order:
Advocated by Presidents and Kings

United Nations' cancerous tentacles secured global lands, rivers, monuments, highways, economics and powers.

Purpose: One World Government for the elite.
Goal: To replace, NOT represent we the people.
How: Sovereign LAW of UN constitution and principles.
Enforced: By a standing UN army.

Suddenly diversity erased, One World Religion embrace, excluding Christians, Jews ruled by law as non-inclusive.

Politics: Elected officials, appointees of UN government.
Compulsory attendance by all nations in a Security Council that denies them status and denies vote.
No nation sovereign. None.
Except One World Order Government.

International Courts compulsory for all citizens of earth.
Human Rights defined by the Supreme UN Power rule.
Economics, Environment, Resources, decided in these courts,
Enforced and allocated by "high level action team" to ALL.

Are the days of Jacob's troubles now at hand with this One World Government advocated by both Presidents and Kings?
Will this dark rule conquer us as foretold? Fear not!
Stand fast!   In Prayer! Occupy!

Soon after is the Sovereign Rule of God!

"The struggle of today,
is not althogether for today - -
it is for a vast future also.

"With a reliance on Providence,
all the more firm and earnest,
let us proceed in the great
task which events have
developed upon us."

Abraham Lincon
From December 3, 1861
Message to Congress

The Collected Works
of Abraham Lincon
Edited by
Roy P. Basler

I Pledge My Allegiance

I pledged my heart and hopes
in the Constitution of this land,
the Bill of Rights, the amendments,
liberty, and religious freedom.
They erode one by one.
Supreme Court rulings:
No God, Churches seized,
appointed president, Wako,
Ruby Ridge,   Ellian Gonzollas ...
Wounded Knee,   presidential perjury.
Govern   ment for all?

I pledge alliance in faith
proven throughout time
in promises kept by
God, witnessed to
the world His
Sovereignty:
creation,
nation
Israel,
in His Son
Jesus Christ,
in whom there is :
Joy, Truth, Liberty, ...
Freedom, Justice and ...
forever life ever lasting for all.

Thundering Hoof Beats

Hear thundering hoof beats
across the desert sands
as nations of the earth
raise dark clouds of war.

Together linked in treaties
like jaw hooks in a beast,
pulling them towards target:
earth's Only International City
by UN decree, Jerusalem.
Then on to Armageddon.
Intention: to obliterate
the City of God and Israel.

The UN condemns Israel.
USA silent. Israel is alone.

"...all nations of the earth
shall be against her ..."

Pray for Israel and all nations!
Clouds of war are rising.
Hear the hoof beats thunder
as they cross the desert sand!

See Them Scatter

They were small in numbers
compared to other parties in the land.
Tragedy struck. They scattered. Fragmented.
They did not stand. Fear scattered them.

Time passed. Fear lessened. They gathered.
In the desert of bewilderment. Reflected.
A spirit of Wisdom came enlightening,
strengthening, binding, and uniting them.

A reformed persecutor of the movement
brought controversy and new wisdom.
Chaos broke out. Angry words. Division.
Outsiders said, "Disorganization. Leaderless.

Each side stood firm in disagreement.

One day with a following of thousands
reformed as a collision united, elevated
by their numbers and convictions,
arose to leadership in the land.

Christians, third parties, living movements.
See them scatter. Scatter to gather.

The past ... the future ... or both?

Feed Them To The Lions Again

"A cultist is one who has a strong belief
in the Bible and the Second Coming of Christ;
who attends Bible studies;

who has a high level of financial giving
to Christian cause; who home schools
for their children;

who has accumulated survival foods and
has strong belief in the Second Amendment;
and who distrusts big government.

Any of these may qualify a person as a cultist
but more than one of these would cause us
to look at this person as a threat

and his family as Being in a risk situation
that qualifies for government interference,"
Janet Reno 6/26/1999 ,"60 Minutes

This is a high ranking government
official speaking who decisions put all
families at risk of government interference.
Does this build your trust in big government?

Is this Profiling? Hate Crime?
Discrimination?

Where is freedom of religion?
What happen to the 2nd Amendment
right to bear arms?

Freedom to read a book of your choice?
What happened to disaster preparedness,
food, water, and shelter for families?

Freedom of speech in the financial
expression of schools, religion, clubs,
political parties?

The Circus Maximus begins again.
Nero calls for gladiators and shouts,

"Bring in the Christians.
Bring in citizens who own arms.
The entertainment is about to begin.
Let them fight to death.
Spectators watch: survivors will
be fed to hungry Lions!

Remember the utterances of words of one
in great power can label good citizens bad,
and in an instant turn good citizens into
criminals and incarcerate them,
as simply as one in great power can pardon
a criminal and in an instant turn a criminal
into a "good" free citizen.

Armed forces remove citizens freedoms
by the direction of great power. We have
witnessed it. Here. Many times.

In practicing your freedom, have you or are
you committing two or more of the qualifying
activities to be labeled a cultist by Reno?

Then YOU, like most of us, ARE AT RISK ...
"for Qualified Government Interference".

POLITICAL

I M P O T E N C E

LEVY ed

IN

MEMORY

OF

GARY ('s)

CONDIT

IS
State of Union
Impeachment
Felony

Jones
Flowers
Lewinsky
Jane Does

Lies
Slander
Adultery
Perjury

The House   Senate
White House   Our House
"Bill" of Rights Constitution
Freedoms   Yours/Mine

DNA
Blue dress
the ORAL office
not sex

The Pledge, The Flag, The Power

I PLEDGE ALLEGIANCE ...
God said swear no oath.

TO THE FLAG
is to swear an oath to a symbol
of power ... to make a promise
to those in positions of power ...

OF THE UNITED STATES OF AMERICA
some states remain commonwealths...
districts, territories, and possessions ...

AND TO THE REPUBLIC FOR WHICH IT STANDS
a republic does not stand for all ...
representative democracy reflects all ...
neither stands for an appointed leader...
both result in an elected leader by vote ...

ONE NATION
we are many nations ... Navaho ... Black ...
Asian... White ... with unequal in rights ...

UNDER GOD
Supreme court rulings removed God:
absent from schools, workplaces...
ruled a church seized by IRS ... 2001 ...

INDIVISIBLE
we are divided by laws, economics,
sex, race, politics, media, power,
taxes, religious discrimination ...

WITH LIBERTY
Liberty is a freedom represented,
reflected, by voter citizens
choosing the leadership ...
Lineage is monarchy ...
Appointment by a few
whether military or political
is dictatorship ...

AND JUSTICE
profiling, salaries, social security
hungry, homeless, the informed...
poor lacking legal defense ...
perjury by a president...
an appointed president...

FOR ALL ...
Four score and twenty years ago...
up to this present day ...
let the blood shed ...
not be in vain ....
testing ...
whether this nation ...
or any nation of freedom ...
can exist with certain
inalienable rights
...FOR ALL

The Time Tunnel

Apparent peace in the Middle East.
History and Present pulsate distrust.
The forces and power of a 4,000 year
feud: Peace for land, Land for Peace.

Blood sons of Abraham divided.
First born Ishmael,
Arab Palestine.
Second born Isaac,
inheritor, Jew.
Descendants:
Arafat and
Netanyah.

They shook
hands toward
peace, control of
Hebron, burial ground
of their forefather, Abraham.
Is it peace?   Or war delayed?

Will time discover a tunnel connecting
the Dome, to temple Mont, to wailing wall,
and ancient temple cause sudden chaos?
A shooting war amidst apparent peace.

Putin's Russia
or
FSB: code for KGB

V ladmier, high in the KGB.
L eaders of Russian underworld
A ssisted his rise with insidious power.
D emocracy changed the KGB to FSB
M aking a change in name only, not policy.
I sreal, Beware!
E comomy failing,
R ussians starving.

P ulling it's fragmented parts together in
U nion: cunning, calculated
T ough, cold secret service man.
I sreal, Beware!
N ames in ancient prophesy make clear,

R ussia will invade the Middle East.
U nder Ezckiel's prophetic cries
S houting down through the generations
S houting through time to the world today.
I sreal, Beware!
A russian army marches undetected.
N ations of the World, Beware!

Election 2000 — Fear Not!

"The only thing we have to fear
is fear it's self"... (Roosevelt, Churchill)

Fear: " A person who represents himself
is a fool"...(a lawyer/attorney)

Fear: "If you vote for a third party you are
just throwing your vote away"... (demo/repubs)

Fear: "So vote for a major party
choose the lesser of two evils"...(demo/repubs)

Why choose evil at all?
Choose evil, get evil!

Psychology: go for what you want,
conqueror fear. It will disappear.

"Ask and you will receive" ... (Bible)

'If you want goodness for our nation
choose goodness for our nation.
Nothing less. Nothing evil.' (Curts)

Let your vote reflect what you want,
unclouded by false fear. Fear not.
Choose the leader of this great land.
voting with spirit, head, and heart.

Four Blind Mice

Four blind mice.
Four blind mice.

See how they run!
See how they lie!

See how they run.
Everything is a tie,

They all ran after the peasants purse
Who cut off their funds at the voting booth.

You've never seen such third party delight
As when they defeated four blind mice.

Third parties run!
Third parties win!

The country needs freedom to survive.
Make the government of the people
come alive.

You'll never see such prosperity in
your life
As the government of the people
comes to life!

Ring freedom ring !
Ring freedom ring!

The Battle Of The Bastard Sons

They entered the ring in fierce opposition
having blocked all other contenders.
In cultic fashion fans rallied support,
the battle of the bastard sons began.

Each shouted lies, truths, half truths
increasing the fervor of the fans.
Blow by blow. The court of contest
bloodied by battling bastard sons.

A peculiar thing: They were illegitimate.
Not favored. Not best. Well promoted.
A purse placed ring side inside arenas
of living rooms, the battling bastard sons.

A supreme blow to jaw. Time out! Stay.
Packed arena. Fans waited. Wondering,
Will it continue? Down for the count?
Which illegitimate contender will win?

Hey, I am in the arena, ticket in hand
so are people from all over this land.
Legitimate contenders! Stick to rules!
We are citizens! We are not fools!

"A SPARK ... FROM GOD"

"Laws just or unjust may govern man's actions.
Tyrannies may restrain or regulate their words.
The machinery of propaganda may pack their
minds with falsehood and deny them truth for
many generations of time. But the soul of man,
thus held in trance or frozen in long night, can
be awakened by a spark coming from God knows
where and in a moment the whole structure
of lies and oppression is on trial for its life.

People in bondage need never to despair.
Let them hope and trust in the genius of mankind.
Science no doubt could, if sufficiently perverted,
exterminate us all, but it is not in the power
of material forces ... to alter the main element
in human nature or restrict the infinite variety
of forms in which the soul and genius

> of the human race can
> and
> will express itself."

Sir Winston Churchill

Democracy

"Democracy is the worst form of government except for all those other forms that have been tried from time to time."

* * *

"It is the people who control the Government ----- not the Government that control the people."

* * *

"The genius ... springs from every class and from every part of the land. You cannot tell where you will not a wonder. The hero, the fighter, the poet, the master of science, the organizer, the engineer, the administrator or the jurist --- he may spring into fame. Equal opportunity for free institution and equal laws."

Sir Winston Churchill

One More Vote Than Russia

What happened to this country, this democracy?
They were strong. Freedom to vote. Their power
slid like Alantis into an ocean of past history.

They had one more vote than Russia.

Two powerful political parties. News media
proclaimed one of them would become president.
The best communication systems of the century.

They had one more vote than Russia.

The people owned the airways,
Media decided what to inform them.
Eighteen parties and thirteen candidates.

They had one more vote than Russia.

Excluded candidates, bewildered voters
switched between the two known parties,
government was "business as usual" and

Freedom Died.   One More Vote Than Russia!

"The opinion which give to the judges the right to decide what laws are constitutional and what not, not only for themselves in their own sphere of action, but for the legislative and executive also In their spheres would make the Judlclarya despotic branch.

...judges should be withdrawn from the bench whose erroneous biases are leading us to Its dissolution. It may indeed Injure them In fame or fortune, but it saves the Republic ... *

Thomas Jefferson

Jefferson's Warnings!

The Supreme Appointment

Title: President Elect.
"George the 2nd" was not elected.
Citizen voter rights unprotected!

It was Seven who declared,
who devined, their votes only
upon this Nation. Who usurped
the Bill of Rights and Constitution.

The title President Elect
is not his crown to wear.
What should his title be?
President Select? Anointed
One? Appointed One? Crown
him George The Second?

The supreme magnificent seven
appointed by presidents before
George's time. Did they know
he was next in line ...

The Supreme Court, their supreme
appointment: Did they serve us?
Did they save us? Or will this
precedence enslave us?

And Then There Were None

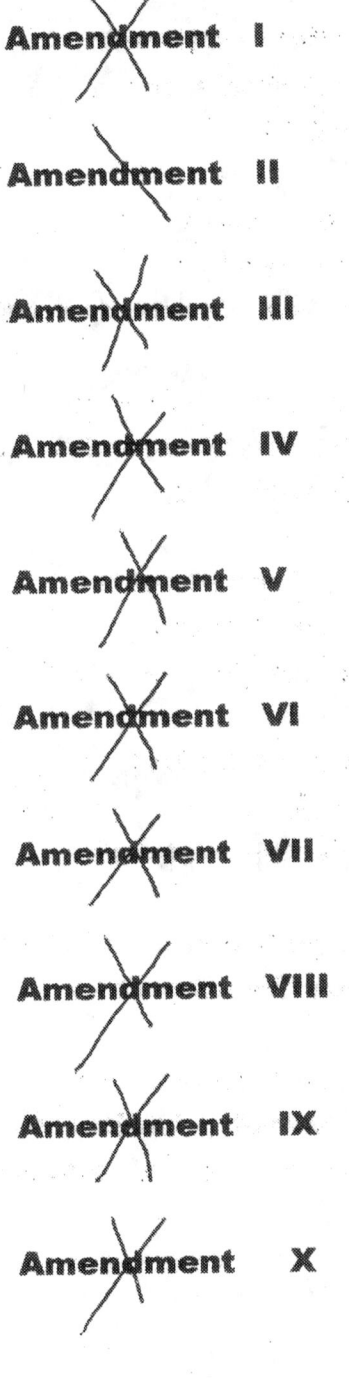

Amendment   I

Amendment   II

Amendment   III

Amendment   IV

Amendment   V

Amendment   VI

Amendment   VII

Amendment   VIII

Amendment   IX

Amendment   X

NONE

**Remember this excerpt
from
Sir Winston Churchill's Quotations on Democracy**

"It is the people
who
control the Government

not the Government
that
control the people."

And I Weep

A friend of mine said:
"Moved by the inauguration service
we drove roadside and wept."

I am repulsed. Inaugural church.
"Everyone's President" by rule.

Vetoed an increase of money for
coal miners widows .... And I weep.

Allowed supreme court ruling for
IRS seizure of a church ... I weep.

Ruled campaign environmental clean up
not necessary for business ... And I weep.

"Leave no child behind": Cut funds: child
abuse counseling, child care. And I weep.

Tax cuts, no budget. Recession!
Preacher of FEAR. And I weep.

Rolling energy blackouts ... the
compassionate consertivitate's
response: solve it your selves.

Injured voters not addressed...
arsenic in water ... all life at risk ...
Fifty-nine days... And I weep.

While it is good to have ecclesia renewing interjective respect, thanksgiving, and celebration as a uplifting moral compass it is sacrilegious, repugnant, and dangerous to impose churchology upon this nation or any nation.

It is a more offensive threat to the separation of church and state than prayer in any classroom(which in my view is good).
It sets a foundational corner stone for a national religion when people accept churchology lead politics.

I remember when people were afraid that John F. Kennedy might lead the nation under the guidance of the pope ...
Be very aware of the leader who believes his is the moral high ground. The truth. The Elite. Who preaches churchology and politics. You see I remember others in history to took that stance. Hitler for example and the Klu Klux Klan.

An Inaugural Revival or The Crowning of King George

While ecclesia is good, renewing,
an interjective respect, thanksgiving,
and celebration as an uplifting
moral compass ...
It is sacrilegious, repugnant, and
dangerous to impose churchology
upon the United States of America
under Presidential leadership.

It sets a foundational corner stone
for a national religion when a leader
bastardizes churchology for self
grandizement and presents it to
the masses vailed as grand regalia.

Be very aware of a national leader
who believe he has the moral "high
ground", power, is ostentatious, and
self serving. With that power law
changes: remember G.W. Bush's
illegal appointment by our Supreme
Court over ruled our Constitution
without objection or protection by
Congress.

There is a dark history in leadership
with others whose moral high ground
was flaunted, bent, and distorted for
the purpose of power. Hitler abroad
and the Klu Klux Klan in the U.S.A.

The Inaugural Revival of The Crowning
of King George the 2nd has already begun
a dark history of Anti - Constitutional Law.

It is Not Religious War

Palestines and Jews Fight
... not a religious war
Muslims and Christians fight
... not a religious war

Islam and Muslims fight
Not a religious war
Islam and Christians fight
Not a religious war.

Arab Nations hate the Jews
not religious war
Politics ....
not religious war.

Catholics and Protestants
not religious war.
Atheists ... hate them all
not religious war.

They all fight each other
but it is not religious war.

Toxic cloud of darkness ...
It is Global Spiritual War!

The Politics Of NOT

Not oil

Not sex

Not lies

Not Daddy

Not political

Not religious

Not contracts

Not alcoholic

NOT TRUTH

Faith Odyssey 2001

An appointed president.
Self-fulfilling recession.
Triangulation politics
Secrecy of policies.

Unemployment
Energy crisis
Stock market falls
Tax refunds

Twin Towers bombed
Undeclared war
Peace on lips
Bombs light sky

Anthrax, Fear
Officials pray
then remove God
across the nation

Faith Odyssey 2001
Hold fast to Truth. Pray.
Do not be deceived nor fear.
God is with you always.

What Happened In September?

What happened to September?
I am trying hard to remember
all that happened September of 2002.

The president announced military action
on Saddamn without congressional
discussion or coalition building.

After criticism he curtsied to protocol.
In the end he got his way.

Large companies collapsed under
the greedy terrorist action stealing
from their stockholders and faithful
employees retirement funds.

Few are punished by the rule of law.
Enron, one prosecution in 300 days.

Congress denies funding for additional
  FBI agent request for 300 new agents
  to defend the US against terrorist.

Unemployment over two million
and no new jobs in sight.

Two million homeless children.

The beginning of a docker's strike,
billions a day gone from the economy.

Instead of an increase in health care
for seniors benefits are cut.

What Happened In September? (Con.)

Crisis after crisis. No recovery.
We grow numb. Is that the intent?
Psychological over load reducing
public ability to respond.

41

Hit them hard. Hit them fast.
Hit them frequently. Inject fear.
Get them off balance.   Move
on fast with "the agenda".

In shell shock, no recovery,
no dissent. Only a sea of
confusion waving flags for
a comforting illusion of unity,
security and strength.

The stock market wreaths
like a dying snake.
Smiles are gone
in the market place.
Middle class investments
evaporate.

I am trying hard to remember
all that took place this tragic
September of 2002 ...
.....   and I can't.

November 2002 Vote

It is a somber November vote.
We can choose a candidate from
our two party system to
continue grid lock on the hill.

In 30 years no prescription drugs,
discrimination of women in social
security benefits, veterans, the poor,
the blaming victims for being robbed
by CEO of companies they invested.

The issues remain the same since
Nixon but the public has forgotten.

A one percent raise for the masses
with congress votes themselves
a pay raise as national unemployment
is on the rise to six percent.

Education, "leave no child behind"
though his swollen belly, unclothed,
neglected, and forgotten.
For some parents working long
hours can't spare the time to raise
them and home is empty bus or car.

We must fight a war for oil, again.
We fight against an evil man who
has not attached us and ignore a
country who has nuclear power.

Long live King George the First
Long live King George the Second
Certainly the rest of us will not live
long nor oil rich lives, nor will our
young in this somber bleak November.

On We March

On we march,
our troops unseen
stalking hidden enemies.

A spiritual war,
good and evil clash
shaking earth's foundation.

On we march,
at the zenith of our power
to rid the world of terrorists.

Unaware of the sudden
slippery decent from
approval to condemnation.

On we march,
nations of the world cry
settle the middle east dispute.

All nations like beasts of burden
with jaw hooks in the mouth
are drawn to Israel, to Jerusalem.

On we march to a veiled valley,
Armageddon.

Where Have All The Bad Things Gone ?

Where have all the bad things gone?
Where did Enron executives go?
The ones that swindled everyone.
Where did life savings go?
The stock market plunge got
everyone ... except a few stewards.
Where did White House ethics go?
They drop their pants, lie to the nation,
insight Congress to finish Daddy's war.
Where did Ben Laudin go,
to met with Saddam underground?
The worlds best intelligence hasn't found.

Where did all the bad things go?
Who benefits from war and woe?
Follow the money. Where does it go?
Look in the bushes you will find
a "cheney" of events lining the pockets
of business allies with spoils of war.
What ever happened to the weapons
of mass destruction? And who's blood
was spilled in the name of war?
Congress voted themselves a raise,
our medical benefits, tax rebates are
are smoke screens, but we see we get less.

God, this country is in a terrible mess.
One thing Jr said that is certainly true,
"This country is in grave danger.."
the grave danger is him.
Where has all the bad things gone?
They are right here where they started
from ... everyone. Our own White House.

Beware! The Eagle Spreads It's Wings

The Golden Eagle spreads it's wings.
The bird of prey with it's great wings
swoops over the weak, conquering,
terrifying, ravaging, killing.

The Golden Eagle spreads it's wings
brings the known world to it's knees,
enslaving, pilfering, and killing,
Roman Peace spread conquering.

The Golden Eagle spreads it's wings.
A slumbering world awoke in horror,
bombs flew, countries conquered,
a race reduced to ash under Hitler's wings.

Policing Peace the Eagle spreads it's wings.
It cast a shadow over 70 foreign lands,
joined by awesome forces: NATO, the UN.
World, Beware! The Eagle spreads it's wings.

A Question Of Honor

It is a question of honoring our American dead:

It was Muslin terrorist who bombed an American barracks in Saudi Arabia ... Africa, an American embassy. Lebanon, the USS Cole.

The US Post Office issued a stamp honoring the Muslim holiday season.

Muslim terrorist using airplanes for bombs: The World Trade Center The Pentagon ... 9/11

Boycott the US postoffice! Don't buy the stamp! It is a question of honoring our American Dead !

Freedom Rings Free

Free speech, movies,
arts, plays, and poetry
express concerns of
thinking minds keeping
watch of changing times.

In censorship they are
removed from public view
so they can not be
communicated to you.

If no one speaks out,
no voice of dissent where
does freedom ring?
Why are voices silent.
Who holds still the bell?

Was freedom sacrificed
on an alter of fear, false
security replacing it?

Where does Freedom ring?

The Bill of Rights
The First 10 Amendments to the Constitution as Ratified by the States
Congress OF THE United States

Amendment 1 :   Congress shall make no law respecting an establishment of religion, or prohibiting the free exercise thereof; or abridging the freedom of speech, or of the press, or the right of the people to peaceably assemble, and to petition the Government for a redress of grievances.

Amendment 11:   A well regulated Militia, being necessary to the security of a free State, the right of the people to keep and bear Arms, shall not be infringed.

Amendment 111:   No Soldier shall in time of peace be quartered in any house, without the consent of the Owner, nor in time of war, but in a manner to be prescribed by law.

Amendment 1V: The right of the people to secure in their persons, houses, papers, and effects, against unreasonable searches and seizures, shall not be violated, and no Warrants shall issue but upon probable cause, supported by , and the persons or things to be seized. Oath or affirmation, and particularly describing the place to be searched.

Amendment V: No person shall be held to answer for a capital, or otherwise infamous crime, unless on a presentment or indictment of a Grand Jury, except in cases arising in the land or naval forces, or in the Militia, when in actual service in time of War or public danger; nor shall any person be subject for the same offence to be twice put in jeopardy of life or limb; nor shall be compelled in any criminal case to be a witness against himself, nor be deprived of life, liberty, or property, without due process or law; nor shall private property be taken for public use, without just compensation.

Amendment V1: An all criminal prosecutions, the accused shall enjoy the right to a speedy and public trial, by an impartial jury of the State and district wherein the crime shall have been committed, which district shall have been previously ascertained by law, and to be informed of the nature and cause of the accusation; to be confronted with the witnesses against him; to have compulsory process for obtaining witnesses in his favor, and to have the Assistance of Counsel for his defence.

Amendment V11: In suits at common law, where the value in controversy shall exceed twenty dollars, the right of trial by jury shall be preserved, and no fact tried by a jury, shall be otherwise reexamined in any Court of the United States, than According to the rules of the common law.

Amendment V111: Excessive bail shall not be required, nor excessive fines imposed, nor cruel and unusual punishment inflicted.

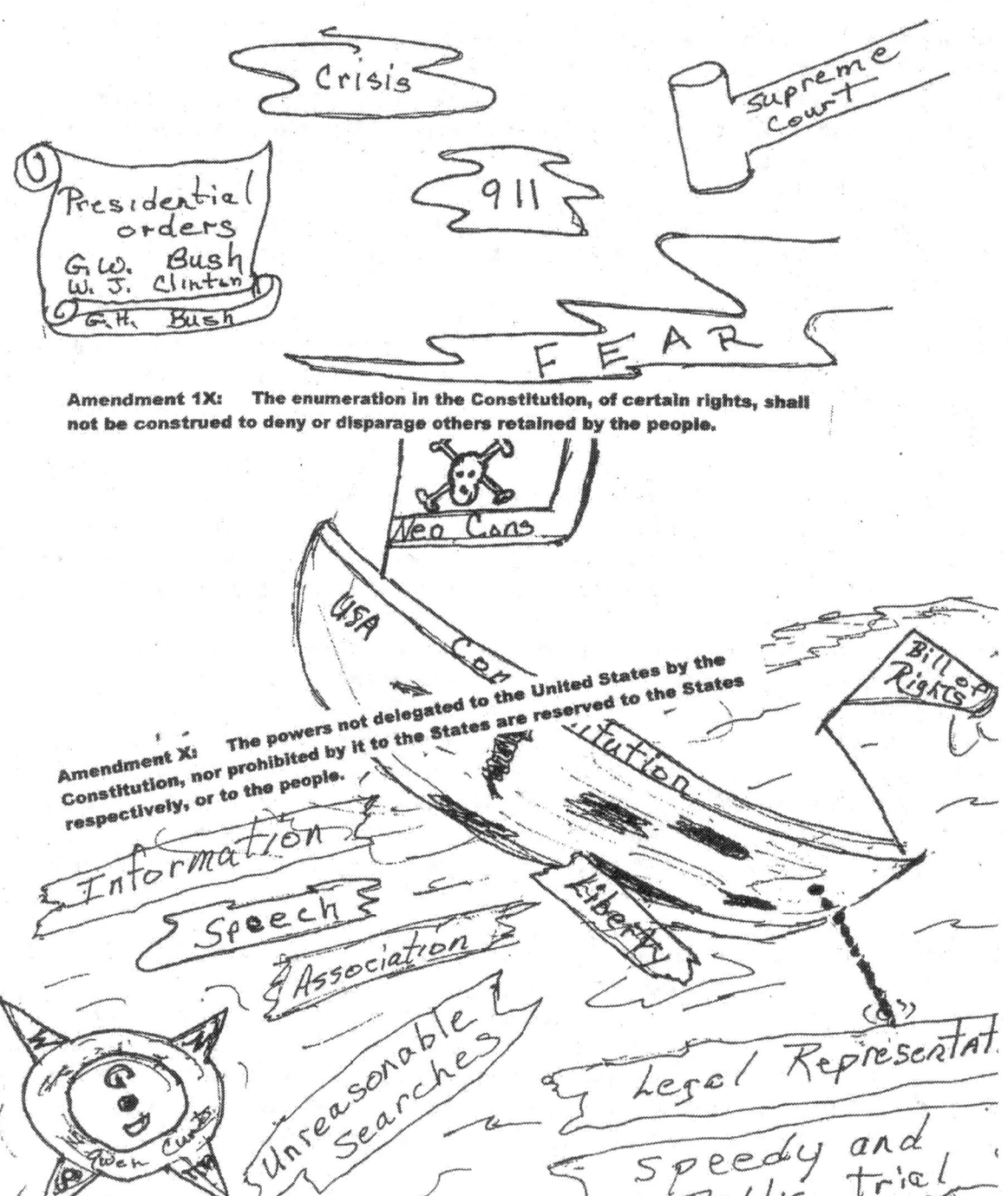

Amendment 1X: The enumeration in the Constitution, of certain rights, shall not be construed to deny or disparage others retained by the people.

Amendment X: The powers not delegated to the United States by the Constitution, nor prohibited by it to the States are reserved to the States respectively, or to the people.

50

"God was walking in the Garden of Eden
showing Satan the whole of creation.
Satan replied, 'Let me put it in Order
for you."

Ram Das

Anthropology of Sovereign Nations

The United States of America
and all nations once sovereign
on planet earth, came under
an authority of sovereign global rule.

This government of Supreme Powers
who's cancerous tentacles secured
lands, rivers, monuments, economics,
highways and rule -- enforced laws
and principles of One World Government
over all the nations.

Suddenly diversity erased, a compulsory
One World Religion was embraced.

Compulsory for citizens of earth:
International Courts for criminal,
justice, economics, environmental, labor ...
Allocated global resources, high level
action team allocated carbon emissions,
universal education cirrocumuli.

Human Rights defined, enforced by
the United Supreme Power. All nations
were required to be part of a Security
Council without vote, without permanent
member status. Elected officials became
elected administrators.

Everyone numbered in the hand
or forehead. Enslaved. The implanted
chip scanned for allocations of fuel,
food, and water. For all resources and
all services.

Anthropology of Sovereign Nations (con.)

Jacob's troubles were at hand.
Jews and Christians died.
No one dared care or help
for their own survival was
was at stake.

The sovereignty of nations
became part of history past.

Then sky a blaze in brilliant white
captured on world channel satellite
the landing of the Atom's force.

There He stood,
the mount of olive split
beneath His feet.

A new rule.
A new millennium.
The Sovereignty of God.

Freedom Postponed

In histories past, their utterances
were loud indistinguishable cries,
faces contorted with pain
and agony of imprisoned spirits
trying to express passions within.

They paced behind high security
fence, razor sharp barbed wire
curled keeping them in and others out.
Their tongues cut out, hands cut off.

These were other times
in other lands. In our own
free speech rings the cry
of war : Operation Freedom.

Postponement of their meeting
guarantees silence for a while.
Postponement to silence to voices
of present day patriotics decent.

Dangerous to present politics.
They swayed public opinion before.
History attests to their success.

It would not go well for democracy
to silence them ... not forever. It would
not be politically correct. Postpone.
Indefinitely. Voices of The Poets.

Hope In Ashes

See the smoke and ashes,
the mountain of debris.
The burning stench of evil,
the human agony.

I see twin towers being built
rising higher than the ones
before made with stronger stuff
than concrete, glass, and steel.

Built by sacrifice and love
in steadfast fortitude
with diligence and prayer.
A bond of human spirit.

Hope rising from the ash
illuminates the world.
Triumph over tragedy,
determination over fear.

I see a united people
laying differences aside.
I see a nation humbled
as a people turn to God.

GENO - ME

GENO - ME, GENO - YOU

Decoding
the mapping
of the human
geno-me
successful.

Now will we cure disease?
or bar the geno-me group
creating medical misfit elite?

Change the genetic sequence
of our maps, geno-me and
geno-you,

before ethics can be established,
ethics based on what?

Be thankful you
were born yesterday
For you are you.

Afflictions, handicaps
have forged heroes
pushing through.

Geno-me and geno-you.
Will their be no heroes too?
Geno-me and geno-you.

The Pro's and Con's of Cloning

Milosevic

MilosevicMilosevic Milosevic

StalinStalinStalin   Stallin   Stalin   Stalin

S t a l i n

Eichman

EichmanEichmanEichman

Saddam Hus

sei m   SaddaHussein

Hitler

Hilter Hilter Hilter Hitler Hilter Hilter Hilter

Eleanor Roosevelt

Eleanor   Eleanor Roosevelt   Roosevelt

Mother Teresa

Mother Teresa   Mother Teresa   Mother Teresa

Chief Joseph

Chief Joseph   Chief Joseph   Chief Joseph

Golda Mier

Golda Mier   Golda Mier   Golda Mier

Gandhi

Gandhi   Gandhi   Gandhi   Gandhi   Gandhi   Gandhi

Digital Angel Versus
Guardian Angel

"Digital Angel', tracking device,
a chip in vaccines contains
medical, economic, political,
religious and family history.

False security rooted in fear;
fear of being kidnapped, sick, or lost.
Fear of neighbors, family and friends
could be terrorist in our midst.

Fear clouds reason. Privacy, freedom,
offerings to a false God, Security.
Guards everywhere for protection.
Suddenly, citizens branded criminals,
descent a crime. Tracker, Digital Angel.
Imprisoned by their protector.

We each have One Guardian Angel
for our security. A legion, 10,000
await our prayer command for
protection in adversity.
Fear Not. Use the resources
God gave for our command.

A Pound of Flesh
(God's Heart)

Humans tortured by Hitler's Dr. Joseph Mangella
repulses the world now as it did then. The Pain.
The word mangle birthed from his death deeds.
Am I glad he is dead?   I am not sure he is.

I fear the spirit of Mangella lives on today.
The Pain. Partial-Birth Abortion sucks infants
brains. They die.

I hear the murderous cries of trafficking for profit
calling out the dismemberment specials of the day.

Eyes $75.OO.   Skin $100.00.   Brain $999.00
Eyes 8 weeks.   Skin 12 weeks. Brain 8 weeks.
Significantly fragmented organs at 30% less,
and 40% off for a single eye. The Pain.

Our fee for service is competitive and attractive.
Fresh Fetal Tissue harvested and shipped,
to you ... where and when you need it. Limbs.
Like a junk car ... their bodies parted out.

Mangella.

Columbine
In
Spring

Columbine in the Rocks is
the first flower to bloom,
the first fruits of Spring,
symbol of Hope,
of beauty
to come.

Columbine students,
like the flower of Spring,
first fruits of a nation,
symbols of Hope,
of beauty
to come.

Columbine students,
death all around,
dark cloud of evil,
buried Hope
in the ground.

A shocked nation,
a stunned world.
A sharing of grief : sadness and tears.
The world reaches out, to comfort, to love,
It's beauty lifting up, empowering Hope.

Why? Littleton, Colorado

A gift of fifteen crosses on the hill
named each victim who's life was taken.
Outcries - anger incite removal.
Fifteen crosses from the hill.

The hill stood barren and bleak.
Anger reverberated mixed with anguish
beyond belief, and shock and sorrow.
Incomprehensible. Who is to blame?

Thirteen crosses reappear anchored
in the ground.
Voices in righteous judgmental indignation
say, Good!
For those two killers don't belong.
They don't belong.
They don't belong nor deserve to be among
their victims.

Separated in death from their victims
as they were separate in life.
They don't belong among their victims.
Those two killers. Who's to blame?
Some said they were the epitome of evil.

Are the rest of us the epitome of good?

Two guilty thieves on a cross.
Jesus in-between.
Guilt lifted up by innocence.

+++

Three crosses stood through time.

"There is a destiny that makes us brothers, None goes his way alone: All that we send into the lives of other comes back into our own.

I care not what his temples or his creeds.

One thing hold firm and fast
That into his fateful heap of day and deeds
The soul of man is cast."

Edwin Markham

Ruby Trilogy # 1
The Land Is Not For Sale!

Definition of a Treaty:
Let's make a deal.
You've got what we want.
We are going to take it.

200 years of Democracy
at work against
Native Americans.

Bureau of Indian Affairs,
Ruby Ridge, Wounded Knee,
Sand Creek, Trail of Tears.
Removal. Confection
without compensation.
Still in place, Genocide
plan.

Mr. Bush the 2nd signed
a bill November 2004
to pay for Western
Shoshone land.

How can this be done?

It is an ILLEGITIMATE
use of presidential power.

The Land Is Not For Sale!

Ruby Trilogy # 2
The Pressure Is On!

The Treaty of Ruby Valley,
1863, replaced Western
Shoshone lands in Nevada.
On them cattle graze for
tribal use.

Government pressure is on
to procure these lands by
what ever means necessary.

Plan: Cattle to be impounded
by the B.L.M., (Bureau of Lies
             and
        Manipulation).

The tribe now faces trespass
fines for cattle on this land,
the IRS threatens seizing bank
accounts and private lands.

Another broken treaty.
Removal on the horizon again.
God help our Native people.

The US government has got
the pressure on!

Ruby Trilogy # 3
Democracy

Remove indigenous people
off their land for profits
of American Corporations.
Recourses: gold, oil,

Does this country need
a trial before the UN
for its continued abuse
of the first citizens
of this land?

Democracy has not worked
in this Republic for Natives.
Why does America fight
for it in Iraq? Land? Oil?

Fight for Democracy in
America. Fight for each
other before we are old,
weak, few in number,
and without resources.

Removal? Democracy?
Ruby Land Is Not For Sale!

We Didn't Wear Feathers

Turbans were the head dress
of choice, long dress or skirts,
pants and shirts, and moccasins.

We were a civilization. We had
councils, a written language,
equality among women and men.

We were agriculturist, farmers,
weaver, herbalist, medicine men.
We were political and democratic.

We adopted others into our house.
We were religious, defenders of
our homes and families.

We were citizens of this land,
good stewards of the environment
and creatures that lived among us.

One day the great white Washington
Father with the stroke of a pen
declared us savages. Removed us.

We didn't wear feathers.

A Cherokee
Walks On The Wind

A Chippewa Song

"The sound is fading away ...
Freedom:
The sound is fading away."

A song of my Chippewa
cousins before freedom was
gone, before the Trail of Tears.

Treaty after treaty broken,
nations were marched along.
Men, women, children died.

The United States government
marched them into unfamiliar
lands without winter provisions.

Tricked and deceived, robbed
of rights, land, possessions.
Broken, spiritually.

2005 ... Broken Bill of Rights

"The sound is fading away ...
Freedom:
The sound is fading away."

One Man's Insight On The Resurrection

"I still can't help wondering how we can explain away what to me is the greatest miracle of all and which is recorded in history. No one denies there was such a man, that lived and that he was put to death by crucifixion.

Where ... is the miracle I spoke of?
Well consider this and let your imagination translate the story into our own time - - possible to your home town.

A young man whose father is a carpenter grows up working in his father's shop. One day he puts down his tools and walks out of his father's shop. He starts preaching on street corners and in the nearby countryside, walking from place to place, preaching all the while, even though he is not an ordained minister.

He never gets farther than an area perhaps 100miles wide at the most. He does this for three years. Then he is arrested, tried and convicted. There is no court of appeal, so he is executed at age 33 along with two thieves. Those in charge of his execution roll dice to see who gets his clothing --- The only possessions he has.
His family cannot afford a burial place for him so he is interred in a borrowed tomb.

End of story? No, this uneducated, property-less young man has, for 2,000 years, had a greater effect on the world that all the ruler, kings, emperors; all the conquerors, generals and admirals, all the scholars, scientists, and philosophers who have ever lived --- all of them put together.

How do we explain that - - unless He really was who He said He was?"

President Ronald Reagan

There Is A Famine In The Land

The people starve.
There is a famine in the land.

A woman reading President Roosevelt's
speech announcing the U. S. entering
W.W.II on a monument cried out,
"they are changing history".
Tears streaming down her cheeks,
her voice cracked as she shouted:

"I was there. I was a little girl.
But I remember what he said.
They left out the most important
words in his speech.
He said we would win
the war with Gods help. "

"There will be a famine
in the land and Gods
Word shall not be heard ..."
(The Bible)

A spiritual Famine.
America Is In The Famine.

Convergence

Convergence occurs when God's ultimate
purpose for humanity is about to take place.
A generation transfer of values from one
to the next unites hearts of parents with
children ending in gratification.
United energy moves to future values
with pains and celebration of new life.

Mortal enemies converged together
in peace aboard Noah's Ark. That march
brought salvation, transformation to
a new level of maturity.

Convergence brings revival, reformation.
United generations move to a Third Way
in the Third Millennium. Liberation, truth.
It will be the end of left and right politics.

As a nation we board the Ark again.
God calls to us. The kingdom is coming.
What will your roles be in the healing
of this land as God's ultimate purpose
for humanity is taking place?

A Prostitute For President

I think we need a prostitute for president.
Someone on the job who follows through.
Where the cost is a known.
Who truly works even flat
on their backs to serve.

Where addenda and intent
are straight forward.
One who's health is
checked and certified
 for the protection
 of the public. We have no
 protection now.

One who when the job
 is finished will walk away
 to new opportunities without
 the need for curtain calls
 and no final climax.

One who wants no further
public exposure ... the work
it self is enough.

Yes I think we need a prostitute
 for president for most assuredly
 he would have no desire to
 prostitute the constitution
 nor the oval office.

Presidential Candidate 2004

For the president of 2004
the precedence is set.

Qualifications:

No psychological profile required.
No one with money or financial clout
refused.

You may rape women,
dodge the draft,
purge yourself in
a court of law, lie to the
American people.
Rent out rooms
in the peoples house
for self profit, pardon
criminals for a bribe.

You may be AWOL for
at least a year from National Guard,
have a drunk driving conviction,
run to the Supreme Court to
win an election unconstitutionally.
Have a religious inauguration.
Strip the land ecologically,
financially, foster pollution,
wage war while people lose wages.

Receive a handsome salary
for the rest of your life.

Honest or poor need not apply.

The Monster Chad

Remember Chad? The Monster Chad.
Took Florida like a hurricane.
Blamed for uncounted citizens' votes.

The chaos of Chad's path
of distruction removed
the rule of the people
to the Supreme decision
of seven in the bushes.

It was a prelude of things
to come, freedoms lost
one by one. Unjust wars,
economic distress, homeland
security, a dynasty dictatorship.

Chad roamed free, unchecked.

He lurks today behind the scenes
to cast his shadow and devour
votes again, November 2, 2004.

What is done to another can be
done unto you.
Make every vote count.

The Eagle And Deciet

The eagle spreads it wings
covering the globe.
The world ordered in oneness.
Unseen far reaching tentacles.

Acting quickly, inducing fear.
Others might attack the nest.
Echelon's watchful eye positioned
for the moment to protect. Then ...

With stealth coercion the eagle
gathered many : hunt or be hunted.
Everyone was tagged with migratory
bands for future rationing of grain.

Blinded by fear the eaglets complied,
begged, demanded their rights, food,
freedom be taken and lined their nests
with illusion. Feathers of protection.

They did not see the veiled heart
of treachery and deceit. Talons
wrapped around them. A sudden
crushing blow. The eagle ate it's own.

A Presidential Write In

Tweedle Dumb, Tweedle Dee
in a mock battle to fool voters
present faux parties.

Their goals are the same.
Give the wealth to foreign lands
Kill off our young people ...
by abortion and draft.

Enslave citizens in poverty
Turn the police force on
patriotic citizens upholding
the Constitution branding them
terrorist or psychriatic dangers.

Block media: short-wave, TV,
radio, magazines, money keeping
others from running.

> One World DisOrder!
> Ketchup or Oil?

A Presidential Write In Would
Improve Our Land.

Cousins For President

We're cousins,
were cousins
running for President.
Kerry and Bush,
10th cousins plus.

We have royal lineage
to Queen Elizabeth.
If you go deeper perhaps
Hapsberg House.

Since Kerry's royalty
ties are closer will he
receive the crown?

Democrat or Republican
it's a Bush this year.
King George or King Kerry?

A Family Tree
Look In The Bushes

Four generations of Bushes have strong Middle East ties.
Great - grandfather: George H. Walker in the Bakian oil fields.

Grandfather: Prescott Bush in the Middle East after World War 11.

Father: George H. W. Bush:
1964   a hireling of the sheik of Kuwait running for U.S. Senate from Texas.
As director of CIA encouraged its involvement in Afghanistan and Pakistan.
Pursued policies making the Middle East primary destination for arms.

1976 cemented relations with the shahs of Iran and Saudi Arabia.
1977 left CIA and became chairman of First International Bancshares
exective commitiee.

1980's as Vice President his role was never clear in the Aran-Contra affair.

1988 - 1992 as President his pivotal role in Iraqgate became clear:
hidden aid provided by the US and it's military built Saddam's army into the
power it became. In addition, the US provided both biological cultures and
nuclear know-how to Saddam's regime along with conventional weapons.
Special prosecutor, Lawrence Walsh asserted Bush had been "in the loop" on
multiple illegal acts. During these years the sons of the president: Jeb, Neil,
Marvin and President George W. Bush lined up business deals
with Saudi, Kuwaiti, and the Bahraini moneymakers.

Family links emerge as the first U.S. political clan to entangle themselves
with the Middle East royal families, oil money and the Bin Ladens
in the 1970's, including George W. Bush.

2000 George W. Bush, President
Connection with Billionaire
Salem Bin Laden and
Banker BCCI insider
Khalid Ben Mahfousz
by Texas businessman
James Bath.

A Nation on The Brink

Minds dulled, eyes blinded by
propaganda, greed, ignorance,
led to slaughter by lying Judas
Sheep who guide and govern.
Big business rules by law, controls
economies, rations goods, disperses
wealth abroad. Sovereignty yielded.
Our compass, God, removed from
public life. Constitution shredded.
Bill of Right stripped by   secrecy.
Fear rules fabric of our lives.

"My people parish for lack of
knowledge," God said in Bible.
No vision, no boundaries, no God -
easy conquest for Strongman's rule.

We are a nation on the brink.

Citizens arise! We have not fallen
yet. Use courage, truth, and light.
Fight for our lives.   Preserve our
way of life. Do it in God's name.

WE, THE PEOPLE!

Who are those folks?   Some without legs,
others without arms, some missing eyes,
ears and half there faces gone.

There clothes are tattered, old from wear,
shoe soles flapping, some looking grungy
disheveled hair, unshaven men.

Certainly they are people from a poor
country, from a very poor country, a third
world country for sure.

No. They are veterans, children, and
women who's blood and toils awarded them
poverty from the US Congress.

Voice Of Dissent

No knowledge of party tenets or principals.
No matter, practicing tenets and principles
changed, no longer recognizable,
from founding written ones.
Both parties agree.   If that is truth ...
is it healthy?   Dysfunctional I'd say.
The leaders profess they are different.
But their purpose is the same.

Where is the voice of dissent?
What is it to disagree?
Today to disagree earns labels like: right
or left, anti-government, subversion, and
seditious.
What would Patrick Henry think?
"give me liberty or give me death".

Where are protesters to gather
where their faces can be seen?
Their voices heard without the hoof beats
of mounted police herding them to obscurity.
They are dangerous. Dangerous indeed.
If they are seen... if they are heard then
there might be dissent ... or worse.
Cause change.   Rule themselves.
Vote in a Third Party breaking up
present two party strong hold.

There is inherent danger when the sights
and sounds of dissent ...of truth it's self
are censored for our minds. We loose power
over our lives, our destiny, our freedom.

I am the voice of dissent.
My mandate: Reform!

The
I A A
is a
bill
drafted
in
SECRECY.

Approved
without
debate.

Provides
funding
for
intelligence.

A
favorite
vehicle of
politicians.

Purpose: the expansion of
GOVERNMENT POWER.

The Fifth Trumpet

The Fifth trumpet calls world
military to enforce restoration,
establishing martial law,
a welcome form of government.

Atomic craters where cities stood,
craters of fear fills hearts to accept
the false hope ... protection.

Establishing the platform for
world power. A governing beast.

A world charter ensuring peace,
disarming individuals and nations.

All fails. All fails.
Peace are the cries.
Promises are lies.
Sovereign nations die.

New government rises from abyss.
The Fifth Trumpet Sounds
announcing the entrance:
a man of order is crowned.

He is the King of Chaos.

A Compassionate Conservative

George Bush the Second,
"watch me to see a living
definition of Compassionate
Conservative".

My four year observation is:

One who buys an office.
Names things the opposite
of what they are. Instills
fear. Appoints daddy's men.
Removes widows pensions,
increases taxes, makes wars,
wants the draft, spends trillions,
grabs social security, promotes
national idenity cards, aliens,
reduces benefits to citizens ...

My definition by observation is:
A Compassionate Conservative
is Neither Compassionate Nor
Conservative.

Hegemony

Neo Cons, powerful folks
striving for U. S.
hegemonic status.

Purpose: maintain an empire
creating democracies , liberal
governments in place of failed
states, oppressive regimes,
threatening U. S. interest.

Results: U. S. unchallenged
by superpowers, immune to
threats, would act as supreme
leader, "Benevolent Global
Hegemony," By U. S.
authority.

This is the PFNAC, Project
For the New American
Century. Global Hegemony
by Neo Conservatives
(Neo Cons).

One World Order.

"Again I admonish you not to be turned from your stern purpose of defending your beloved country and its free institutions by any arguments urged by ambitious and designing men, but stand fast to the Union and the old flag."

Abraham Lincoln August 31j1864 Speech to the 148th Ohio Regiment

The Collected Works of Lincoln
Edited by
Roy P. Basler

Project for New American Century

Secret order of elite. Unipolar
Government, One World Order in
Disguise. Neo-Conservatives.

Our sons and daughter march
on battlefields we don't belong
across oil fields in Middle East.
They die. Their families destitute.
Heaven help you if a limb is blown
off when in the heat of battle you
step beyond the battle line.
Two wars, more to come. In the
name of democracy we make war
under the guise of making peace.
In the meantime somebody is
getting powerful and rich.

Create a New Pearl Harbor, 911,
the illusion of terrorism, results, fear.

Postpone the poets conference.
Freedom of Speech. I have
experienced several of my political
writings removed from public view
which contained truthful
enlightenment of secrecy of laws
and bills passed by Congress.

Free press threatens their agenda
They pirate away the Internet in
the name of protection, reading
our mail. Make banks report
withdrawals and deposits over
a certain amount. Privacy, past.

The eyes and ears of a Shadow
government, an Under government
are every where ... even chips in
clothing. Injections. Soon TV.
Every citizen take a psych exam.

A citizen maybe arrested
and detained without council,
and notification.
It is permissible to use
torture on any citizen as long
as an organ is not injured.
Wonder how they define organ?

I could be arrested today
without council, falsely charged,
labeled a terrorist by our government,
imprisoned for life or worse, tortured
legally by our present law ...
and so could you.

The Patriot Act has made it legal to
remove our rights so that Patriots
can not act nor speak out against
the removal of our freedoms without
engendering the dangers of being
labeled criminals, terrorists, insane
and subsequently arrested.
This is not protection. This is Hitler's
regime revisiting planet Earth.

How can giving up a freedom
make you secure and free? It
never worked for citizens of
any other country.
Increase defense, taxes, war.
Does this sound like peace?
When they say democracy think slavery.
For it will be.
When they say peace know war is on
the very horizon of the day it is said.
When they say prosperity, know they
mean theirs, and you are headed for
debtor prison or worse.
When they say "last resort"
know they mean only resort,
the one they want.

I implore you fellow citizens,
patriots with the heart of our
founding fathers and mothers:
When they point one way quickly
look in the other and see what
truth you are being distracted
from. Do not believe an accuser.
Seek the truth. The truth beyond
the shouts, waving flags, and spin.
It lies somewhere in a dark hidden
place but you will find it. A place
none of us want to go and many
died so we would not have too.

We must seek the truth.

Nothing is what it seems to be.
Lies and deception abound.
Surround us. We are covered in
a dense fog of spinning lies, blanketing
TRUTH so it cannot be known for if TRUTH
were known than deception would be
OVERTHROWN.

This is the Program of a New American
Century (PNMC), of Neo-Conservatives,
their plan for our country, for the world.

"When the freedom they wished
for most was the freedom from
responsibility,
then Athens ceased to be free
and was never free again."

Edith Hamilton

Totalitarianism for Security

Begin with a large amount of propaganda. Hitler said, "the bigger the lie the greater the belief".

Pass laws to use against citizens, demonize those who oppose them as unpatriotic or "your either with us or against us," (Bush 11)

Remove and silence those in opposition. No one has the power or force to assist individuals in opposition.

Expunge liberties of citizens:
Freedom of Association: government monitoring without suspecting criminal activity. Private Internet, churches, et.

FREEDOMS LOST

Freedom Of Information: Closed hearings, secrecy. No charges, no public records to question.

Freedom Of Speech: prosecution if subpoenaed and charged as relaying information on terrorist investigation.

Right To Legal Representation: Government may monitor and deny lawyer to any citizen accused of crimes.

Freedom From Unreasonable Searches: The Government May Search and Seize Americans' papers and effects without probable cause to assist in a Terror Investigation.

Right To A Speedy Trial: Government may jail Americans indefinitely without a trial.

Right To Liberty:
Americans may be jailed
without being charged or
without being able to confront
witness against them.

* * * * * * * * * * * * * * * * * *

When I began this book William Jefferson Clinton
was President. I was Free to speek out, to write
criticizing my government and it's officials.

Mr. Clinton was busy designing both the Patriot Act
and the Department of Homeland Security. Bush 11,
appointed President, instituted both plans designed
by Clinton.

I have lost my rights and so have you. Some of my
writings have been expunged from and Internet site.

I live in fear of my own government. I will seek
freedom of publication in another country to avoid
being banded from publication in the U. S. I fear
reprisal that could punish other innocent parties,
family, friends.

Yet I do what I must. I remain a patriot of old,
like Patrick Henry, "give me liberty or give me
death". I believe death or worse could happen.

Give me my Freedoms in the Constitution of
the United States and the Bill Of Rights.

"It is your business to rise up and preserve the Union and liberty, for yourselves, and not for me. I desire they shall be constitutionally preserved."

Abraham Lincoln
From February 11, 1861
Reply to Governor Morton

The Collected Works
of Abrahm Lincoln
Edited by
Roy P. Basler

The Day America Died:
12/09/2004

The President, House, and Senate gave the following power to the Federal Agency, Homeland Security which is an oxymoron and appropriately should be called Homeland Confinement.

This Federal Agency will now dictate to regulate the information collection of citizens on drivers licenses, birth certificates, biometric markers by the Federal government. The data base itself will be maintained by Homeland Security.

No child will be allowed school enrollment nor State or Federal benefits without it. A Homeland Security registration Birth certificate. However, ILLEGAL ALIENS will NOT have to meet these requirements as sanctioned by the President, the House, and Congress.

By a ruling of The Supreme Court, Federal and State Law Enforcement authorities have the RIGHT to REQUEST identification from any AMERICAN which will include the individuals social security number on the drivers license.

Banks and Credit cards will require only the drivers license to purchase or transact business for the balances will be available in real time and immediately accessible.

A chip in the forehead or hand is next folks to prevent "final" identity theft ... 666.

Homeland Security will maintain a separate data base ID for citizens boarding airplanes as did the Soviet Union and Nazi regimes, the internal passports.

"People willing to trade freedom for temporary security deserve neither and will lose both", Benjamin Franklin.

Have we lost both?

Election Day

Election Day in the USA.
Will it be held this year or
will a homeland disaster
result in Martial Law
postponing an election?

I find it odd Iranians fly
planes into Twin Towers
and we make war on Iraq.
What are the odds that
no one would be in that wing
Pentagon when the air plane
crashed in its front lawn.
Security cameras every where
no video tapes to review.

If Canada bombed us would
we make war on Mexico?

Skull and cross bones, secret
orders on American soil, the
people know not what they
are about. Terrorist cells aimed
at One World Order, is that what
their are about. Who investigates
them for our national security?

"I am a WAR TIME president",
George W. Bush said as he
strutted about. Skull and Bones,
banks and oil, will elections
continue on American soil?

Deep Roots: It Happened In Iraq

The Land of Shiner, Mesopotamia,
The Garden of Eden, rich with
artifacts and Bible History.

The land where many Bible folks
lived from Abraham, Noah,
and numerous others. The "hand
writing on the wall", it all
happened in Iraq.

No weapons of mass destruction,
no chemical war fare, no present
danger there. No connection with
911 both Tony Blair and Bush said.

Bombed, plundered, human history
now erased from this deep rooted
desert place where the history of
God's chosen people began.

Why did this invasion take place?
Was it just for the riches and the oil?
"Not a religious war", Bush said.

Was it a spiritual war perhaps.
The devil made his first appearance
here. In addition the greatest
revival in history took place.

Deep Roots: It happened in Iraq

Star Wars

Control weather, control the world.

Bombs of pin point accuracy cause:
droughts, floods, earthquakes, tidal
waves, erupting volcanoes, without
the world knowing, weather warfare.

Electromagnetic fields of land, sea,
and air jammed by stronger electromagnetic fields replace, redirect.

Whales in confusion, beached,
die on Florida's coast. Override,
remote control airplane flight
to designated targets, pin point
accuracy. Military science.

ELF ... Extremely Low Frequency
radar. Sudden climate change.

HAARP ... High-frequency Active Aural
Research Weapon, mass destruction,
New World Order U.S.A.   Star Wars.

It's A Matter Of Economics

Imagine you are a large investor
in a giant European corporation.

Euro value grew strong,
dollar fell below the Euro.

It would be economic suicide to
advocate strengthening the dollar
by bringing businesses, jobs to the
the states decreasing your profits.

Now you are President. A large car
company in the states employing
families claims a million dollar loss.

Would you "compassionately" say
"you'll just have to become more
competitive" allowing everyone
involved to be jobless.

Where are the uplifting words
from the leader on the hill?
Where is concern for the people?

It is probably "conservative".
You and your cohorts on the hill
would conserve and increase
your investments and control.

Since this is true. It is a matter
of economics: the Euro increases
while the dollar shrinks.

A Revolution or A Revelation?

When elected officials truly represent
The People
When they are morally and ethically
responsible in their offices carrying out
their duties by the powers invested to
them by The People,
interceding for the Rights and liberties
of The People ...

Then No Blood Is Shed.
No Revolution Is Necessary

When Congress stands fast upholding
the Constitution and the Bill of Rights,
the foundations of our free society,

Then No Blood Is Shed.
A Revolution Is Not Necessary

Remove vision, remove religion,
remove history, remove economics,
remove symbols, remove the moral
compass and liturgy of a society,
split families, remove to foreign lands ...
they flounder, weaken, and will cease
to exist.

Only pillars in fields of decade stench,
stubble, and ash remain in clouded
confusion, disappear, anarchy or
obedient submission.

America allowed prayer removed
from schools, Ten Commandments
removed from public view,

life removed abortion
life remove undeclared war,
Bill of Rights removed,
Godly entertainment removed,
history removed, economics
removed from our treasury.

Immoral leadership stayed.

Instead of feeding our minds, our
bodies, and souls on healthy
sustenance we choose hate,
abandonment, drugs, lies,
stealing, pervasive entertainment,
disrespect for life and turned away
from the founding Father of our
Government.

God, himself.

A Revelation Is Needed: We,
The People, are responsible.
 We need to turn our hearts
and minds back to God for the
healing of this land.

We need to remove power
from public officials who rape us
of our rights, liberties, our
Constitution, our history.

No Blood Shed Is Necessary.
No Revolution.

A Revelation Is Needed:
The People Turning Back
To God.

The Preservation Of England

The English Parliament brought formal charges
against King Charles Stuart, (Charles 1), as a tyrant.

One who acted contrary to the limited power
of King in the Magna Charta and written or
unwritten Constitution.

Guilty of Treason and Perjury, neglecting to perform
the duties of an absolute Oath of Office of King.

The Kings powers are limited for the benefit of the
People to preserve their rights and liberties.

Charles put his interest before the interest of the
People overturning their rights and liberties.
Causing wars denying people liberties, spilling
innocent blood, ruined families, exhausted the
public treasure.

Parliament acted protecting the People.
Charles was beheaded January 30, 1649,
the People of England's rights and liberties
are preserved for another 356 years.

For a moment substitute the following:

1. U. S. Congress for Parliament,
2. President George Bush11 for Charles 1,
3. U.S. Constitution and Bill of Rights for
     the Magna Charta, and the rights and
     liberties of both people.

The preservation of the rights and liberties
of the People of England and the _____
of the rights and liberties of the people of America.

Freedom Rings

When we agree to disagree
Freedom Rings like Carillons.

When we take responsibility
for our economics, health,
investments, personal security,
sweet freedoms Rings.

When we criticize our government
without fear of being incarcerated
 ... Freedom Sings

When morel leaders lead
and uplift the spirit of the land
in freedom we are invincible.
Freedom Sings.

When we honor and obey
the laws of God we are
prosperous and freedom rings.

When Good People
rise to the occasion,
grab hold the rope, in
God's name pull till
the clapper rings large
wrippling waves of medloic
sound and pray God heal
this land then ...
 Freedom Rings.

Israel Gone ...

12/08/05, New York, UN nations
met. A festivity, "... solidarity..."
 A new map unveiled flanked by
UN and PLO flags revealed their
solidarity intent. Palestine ...
from the Jordan River to the sea.
Silence honored lives lost in the
Palestinian cause ... Terrorists.

No Israel. No Jewish state. What
God decreed wiped off the map.
No outrage against this act.
"all nations of the earth shall turn
against her" the prophet said.

Pray for the leaders, the people
of all nations. Their hearts are
hardened against the Holy One.

The Lord God will prevail. Israel,
Jerusalem will survive. Jesus
will return. For our mercy,
"it is written".

Psalm 2005 For America

Oh Lord, my God, I give thanks
to You for the founders of this
country who sought Your Wisdom
raising up this nation. Imperfect
sinners. Learning. Struggling.
Suffering. Praying. Benefactors
of Your mercy. Your love. Your
freedom, riches, and strength
making this nation a beacon
of Your hope to the World.
We praised and honored You.

Lord, I cry out to You. My heart
is in agony. My nation, its'
leadership, my people no longer
seek your Wisdom. With hearts
of self centered sin turned away
from You. They have shut You
out of schools, courts, history.
They mock and profane You.
We crumble under our sins.
Freedom, riches, strength wane.

I beg You, merciful God: turn our
hearts back to serve, honor, obey
and praise You our Redeemer!

Preachers Of Fear

Hear them, preachers of fear.
Doomsville, Armageddon. Terrorist.
Eroding the confidence of a nation.

Be afraid. These are dangerous
times, they say, weaving, spinning
fear into the fabric of our lives.
Shredded of rags of rights shackled
to homeland securely by illegal
orders, by laws of treason.

Give us your rights, for protection.
We strip search you, citizen, for your
protection, monitor your e-mail,
bank accounts, telephone. Arial
grid surveillance of your home.

They shout aggression, becoming
the aggressor. Claim crisis after
crisis. Weapons of mass distraction,
weapons that are not there.

Never before in our US history
has leadership TOLD this nation
to FEAR.   NEVER.   Leadership in
history past STRENGTHENED us.

We live in dangerous times at
home when we are forced by
law to enter the dark bowels of
hell and ingest the spirit of our
leadership, Evangelists of Fear.

Election 2008

Here is a voter's slate.

Demo-publican

Re-democrat

Publican-demo

Public-crate

Republican

Democrat

No matter how they package it, adding New or any other suffix, prefix, in a skirt or in pants all of the above are the same one party hoping to fool We the People once again. Thirty years of grid lock on the hill. Lets end it.

Do a Presidential Write In.

It is the right time to fool them. It is our finest moment to vote a **THIRD** party into the Presidency to strengthen this republic. It is the Hope we have to regain our Rights, preserve this nation.

Demand TV coverage at the polls so if citizens are denied or obstructed from exercising the right to vote the viewing public knows. And if such a thing occurs again, demand your fellow citizen's vote be counted under any circumstance. We must stand for each other to succeed.

Hold prayer groups before the election. Let the spirit of God guide you in prayer. God bless you and God bless America.

Hope

God is a forgiving God when nations repent
and turn back to Him. He heals them. He
heals their land. He says, "Fear Not".

We need to take responsibility for our freedom
and NOT trade it for false security. We need to
utilize that power, it belongs to We the People
BUT for only as long as we fight for it at home.

We must have knowledge. Know the
Constitution and the Bill of Rights.
Know the records of office holders.
The truth, the facts are not on the surface.
Dig them out. Over 150 people ran for
president in the election. There are many
parties, most blocked from our view, rules
made up by the "two party system.   Know
who supports our Constitution and our
Bill of Rights.

Develop study groups, divide assignments,
find facts, share them. Know your neighbors.

Bush wanted us to keep an eye on each
other and report anything suspicious
(Hitler wanted that too).

But I say share with your friends and neighbors
what is happening to you. There is no strength
in isolation.   Share what is happening to other
citizens like Native Americans whom Bush
wants to Remove again. Pensions cut. Health
care cut. Gas, groceries, jobs. And DO NOT
believe rumors about each other. Find truth.

Hope (con.)

Stand up for each other. Help each other.
Use the laws of the land. Remember anyone
who changes them is committing treason if
your Constitutional Rights are forfeited.
                    Unite.

Hope is in us. The people of God. Know what
He has to say about nations and boundaries,
droughts and earthquakes, and other things
Read His book. See what you think. Wisdom.

We, as individuals and as a nation, have a great task
before us.   Hope takes an active form.   Our safety,
our security lies in the Constitution and the Bill of
Rights guarded by We the People.

With God's help, we will get them back.
            Unite. Go forward!

            And
        above all

        FEAR NOT !

Foreword

It is my hope now that you have finished this book we all move forward anew being vigilant of those whom we put in places of power.

For it is we, the people, who are in charge of Guarding our Constitution, the Bill of Rights, both protecting and respecting our individual rights and diversities.

If those whom we have put in power to entrust our liberties abuse them then we must stand together and remove them. Remove them from power not only for our own sake but for the very existence of freedom.

Go forth with open eyes, open ears, and in your faith tear down the veils of deception and spin masters. For we do not want them to inherit the earth.

It is to you, the reader, that I am indebted to for your participation in the adventure of this book and greater yet, in this adventure we call freedom.

Madeleine L' Engle said in her book, <u>Walking On Water</u>, that an author must get out of the way and become "a servant of the work". It is in that spirit I sign off as:

"A Servant Of The Work"

Bibliography

1. Hosea   <u>The Bible</u>   Chapter 6
   Created by God

2. Dwight David   1961   Farewell Address to the Nation
   Eisnehower   The Military -- Industrial Complex

3. John F   1963   Commencement Address at the
   Kennedy   American University ... Pax Americana

4. Abraham Lincoln   <u>The Collected Works of Abraham Lincoln</u>
   Edited by Roy P. Basler

5. Abraham Lincoln   <u>The Collected Works of Abraham Lincoln</u>
   Edited by Roy P. Basler

6. Sir Winston   <u>The Wit & Wisdom of Winston Churchill</u>
   Churchill   James C. Humes

7. Sir Winston   <u>The Wit & Wisdom of Winston Churchill</u>
   Churchill   James C. Humes

8. Thomas Jeffersons   <u>Citizens Rule Book</u>
   Warnings!   Edited by Webster Adams

9. Sir Winston   <u>The Wit & Wisdom of Winston Churchill</u>
   Churchill   James C. Humes

10. The Bill Of Rights   Constitution Party web site
    www.constitutionparty.com

11. Ram Das   I do not know where I obtained this
    quote of Ram Das

12. Edwin Markham   <u>The Family Book of Best Loved Poems</u>
    Editor David L. George

13. Chippewa Song   <u>The Trail Of Tears</u>
    Gloria Jahoda

14. Ronald Reagan   One Mans Insight On The Resurrection
    a note by President Ronald Reagan

15. **Abraham Lincoln**   **The Collected Works of Abraham Lincoln**
                             Edited by Roy P. Basler

16. **Edith Hamilton**   **The Echo of Greece**
                             by Edith Hamilton

17. **Abraham Lincoln**   **The Collected Works of Abraham Lincoln**
                             Edited by Roy P. Basler

18. **Abraham Lincoln**   **The Collected Works of Abraham Lincoln**
                             Edited by Roy P. Basler

19. **Madeliene L' Engle**   **Walking On Water**
                             Harold Shaw Publishers, Wheaton, Ill.

*   **All presidential quotes may be found by going to
    www. presidents name library.com**

** **All quotes appear in the bibliography in the order they appear
    in this book.**

Postscript

The day I completed this book Congress passed a law that will now require every U.S. citizen to have and carry a National Identification Card.

National Identification Card

Rest assured everything is secure.
Every citizen must have a National
Identification Card. A Hitlerian tactic.

This will assist our government
in knowing, controlling all we do.

There will be no foreign terrorist
here. Terrorism will be internal.
Papers please. National I D.

Why were France and England safe?
No 911, no anthrax there. External
terrorism is not our threat.

A faux republic, bogus democracy,
foisting a warped system on other
nations by force, conquering.

A government that decides what
writings are in good taste, instructs
writings like this to be erased.

Hovering helicopters erase hard
drives. National Identification.
Feel Freer? Safer? God Help Us!

"The people are the masters

of both Congress and the courts,

not to overthrow the Constitution

but to overthrow the men

who would pervert it."

Abraham Lincoln